A MOTHER KNOWS HER CHILD

A MOTHER KNOWS HER CHILD

Poetic Meditations from Mary

Linda Beatrice Brown

Women and Wisdom Press

Also By Linda Beatrice Brown

Poetry:
A Love Song To Black Men

Fiction:
Rainbow 'Roun Mah Shoulder
Crossing Over Jordan
Black Angels

Non-Fiction:
The Long Walk
Belles of Liberty

Cover Photo: *"The Manger"*
Photograph by Gertrude Kasebier, 1903
Cover Design: Gabrielle B. Beard and Brandy Pickrell
Mother Mary Watercolor and Graphic: Linda Beatrice Brown

Designed and Published by
Women and Wisdom Press
*A Creative Empowerment Project of
Women and Wisdom Foundation
Greensboro, North Carolina*

Women and Wisdom Press

www.womenandwisdom.com

Second Edition
978-0-9888937-3-3
Printed in USA

DEDICATION

To The Divine Mother

Table of Contents

Preface

I offer these poems and meditations to all of us, in humility and gratitude that we may see in the Mother's face a way to heal ourselves. If you are reading this you know that we are in a time of massive change on our planet, a critical turning point for the earth and all her children. It is only through the heart that we can become who we are meant to be, that we can see ourselves as She sees us.

These meditations come forth as part of a great tide of energy on the planet today from Beloved Mother, whose command I prayerfully received and now pass on to you.

"Write my face upon the world.

I am the face of all women. Those who see them see me. I am every woman lost and every woman found. I am here. I have always been here. The Spirit of the Mother must rain down love. It must hold our earth and rock the pain away. It must water the earth in tears of consolation and wash its wounds with saving grace. I am here. I grieve with every mother who has ever lost a child.

I am your stillpoint in the Heart of Hearts. I stretch out my arms to you, my heart burning within. I am the Sacred Heart and you are my children. My story is your story. I am waiting for your love."

Linda Beatrice Brown

July, 2014

Finding Our Divine Mother
In Her Humanity

In the midst of our theologies and speculations, we long for an intimacy with our spiritual legacy. "To be in the world and not of it" is the mandate. Yet often we have felt the Divine Mother was far removed from our earthly reality.

This collection of poems—and I am tempted to say "these dialogues with Mary"—bring her human reality into a focus that celebrates and empathizes with her, walking with her through the harsh and sublime passages in her life. From the young girl who became the vessel for a message that would change the world to the aging Mary, Linda's poems explore the very nature of sacrifice. As I read I was alternately in tears and awe, often at the same moment.

This is not a Mary removed from the struggles of womankind. This is the earthly mother who models surrender to her spiritual mission, even when her heart is breaking; the mother who year by year watches the mystery unfold the destiny of her child, knowing all along its inevitable ending.

Through Linda's intuitive imagination and extraordinary writing skills, we experience Mary as she observes with keen insight the reactions of those around her, from Joseph to the mobs, to the disciples debating a new beginning after those terrifying days of an ending. We gain insight into her suffering, sometimes her anger. Through it all we hear her sacrifice and her aloneness. There was for her no map to follow, no Easter promise to ease the pain.

Each of these poems is a gem to be treasured. Together they shape a powerful and poignant portrait of a woman who has beckoned to us through two thousand years. They will be read and reread, providing insight, comfort and illumination. As we are led gently and firmly to view Mary's spirit expressing through her humanity, we are brought closer to our own.

Gloria Karpinski
Author and Spiritual Teacher

Poetic Meditations from Mary

SUN BLIND

I

They say if you look at the sun full on you will go
blind.

There is no way to see him without protection.
Beware the Man of Fire,
for the trees he walks by will glisten and burn.

Do not come near unless you want to be struck in
the heart by lightening and live in the storm.

His mother's milk was unencumbered Light,
her lullaby a warning.

Walk this way, she said, and the stars will turn
at your command
while men forget your real name.

Beware the Man of Fire.
There is no safety there.

II

She did her best. She told him true.
The world hid dangers unimagined.
Could a boy in the temple know that his mouth
would get him killed?

It was only later, when they began that long walking
from town to town,
it was only then, when sidelong looks and sneers and
a stone or two was thrown,

It was only then, in those little tight towns,
that his mother's wisdom rang in his ears.
"Men will forget your real name," she had warned,
"though stars turn at your command."

III

They say if you look at the sun full on you will go
blind.
They never looked into his eyes.
They never could have.
Alive with Love he was a living target.

Beware the man of Fire.
There is no safety there.

Blinded by Love
You will stumble down his path and fall,
silently, splendidly,
into a swirl of perfect knowing.

THE GOLDEN FEATHER

I do not know what manner of bird could shed a
golden feather in my closet.
At night it shimmers, but I tell no one.

~~~

My sisters lingered at their fire, singing softly and
dreaming of young men,
so many stars above it seemed you could scoop them
with a gourd.
I asked permission to go to my bed. It had been a
day of bread making, pounding millet, kneading, and
tending hot ovens.

Their voices softly murmuring were a lullaby. I was
asleep almost at once.
I slept like a child, sure of safety, sure of love.

Deep into the night, I opened my eyes.
Awake, I was standing on a great hill. Far below me
was a sea, a vast, unending sea of ages.

A white wind held me, surrounded me, fierce, wild.
It roared, and in curious words
I did not understand, it sang to me.

It did not threaten; it did not frighten. It blew into
my face and made my hair a wild diadem.
What did I know of angels?
What did I know of visions?

Out of the wind came a sound, words that meant
"babe, child of the Most High, Mother of God."
I understood the words.
I didn't understand the words.

What did I know of angels with wings of white fire
and eyes like lightening?
And all the while I stood on the edge of
that great hill,
not afraid of falling, not afraid of anything.

With a voice like liquid silver it sang to me
and I sang back, in that mysterious tongue
about my soul, about the Most High,
singing of a child in strange words I didn't know
I knew and now I don't remember.

"Mary," the wind called, "Mary." I did not awaken
then, for I was not asleep.
I closed my eyes. Sleep like a trance descended.

Later I was different. For days I couldn't speak.
I wept, dropped things.
My vision blurred.

I had a dream, I told myself.
Perhaps I have a demon.
But I knew there was a child coming.
How I knew I cannot say. I stood on a hill in a great
wind, and heard strange music.

I do not know what manner of bird could have shed
a golden feather in my closet.
At night it shimmers. I tell no one.

SAVED

This dry and windy day I draw water from the well.
I slip the rope about my arm, make sure that it is tight
around the jar.
The empty water jar bumps soft against my womb.
Everyday I am sent to draw water,
And every day I feel it more.
When will they know?

I pull my garment so it hides the child in me.
Wind whips around my skirts, swirling up dust. I
watch my body every day. The child is coming, a glory
babe, the angel said and it is time for me to wed.

An angel put it in me. It is my truth. Not like this
wind, another wind it was. A wind from Heaven. If
I said it, they would laugh or worse.

There are women at the well, for the early morning
draw. I know them all and they know me, but I am
not the same. I will never be the same.
Soon they will know, my mind warns me.

To die by stoning. That is what they do to girls like
me. I know the law. The law is clear.

I let my jar down slowly. The gust is strong and I need
both my hands. My garments part, the women look.
 hear the vessel hit the water, feel my heart is in that
jar. I draw my water, loop the rope around my arm,

steady my water jar on my head.
They are very quiet now but they are looking.

It is an unfair wind. An angel put it there. And they
are looking.
I take my time in order not to drop the water jar. And
was I born to bring this shame to those who love me?
An angel babe. An angel babe.
To die by stoning. Both of us, both of us, the
sweet babe never born.

~~~

Elizabeth my cousin knows. She understands.
A great wind came and left me with a babe from
God. That's all I know. They say that Joseph, son of
Jacob, is to marry me.
He picked me from the others.
This Joseph is a righteous man they say. I pray that he
is generous of heart and kind. I pray. I pray.

~~~

His eyes go through my skin and he is raging.
This Joseph is a righteous man.
I know he wants to strike me but he doesn't.
I get down on my knees and swear that I am pure.
I tell my truth.
A babe of glory. That is all I know.

He is not moved. He turns and leaves me in the dirt.
To die by stoning, both of us, the sweet babe never
born.

An angel came and now I am undone.
I am undone.

~~~

Morning comes. I tremble in my bed.
To die by stoning. Where is my angel now?
Where are the great wings and the silver music?
An angel came and I said yes to God and that is all I
know. And now I am undone.

My sister enters laughing tears.
"Saved," she calls out. "You are saved!"
"This Joseph had a dream," she says, "a dream from
God, and you are saved!"
Her tears are mixed with mine, and then the child
laughs, my child in me laughs, such laughter that the
golden temple bells that play their airy tunes are put
to shame.
I hear him in my heart.

THE BROKEN BIRD

I

The day of the broken bird I saw him watching it,
The bird hardly bigger than the shell it had hatched
from.
He didn't know I was watching.
I often did that, stood in the doorway to see that he
was not in danger.

He was hardly a boy yet, still,
Not a baby anymore.

The bird's broken wing was dragging.
I saw him looking, wondering. It had fallen from the
tree behind our house.
Never to fly, never to live.
Its older brother may have pushed it out.
They did that sometimes to take food for themselves.
Like some men I knew.

I saw him looking at the creature with those eyes,
eyes that seemed from birth to hold the night and its
ten million stars.
I saw him put one tiny finger on the creature's downy
feather.

It rose with unbroken flight to the nest above.
Returned home to live again.

II

I must have felt it even then.
Fear barely whispering my name,
So gentle, tender even, "Mary, Mary."

It was a yellow day, that day of the broken bird.
I wouldn't have noticed, but for a leaf turned the
wrong way on the tree,
The soup slightly off, so that his father left his bowl
untouched.
That was the way it was in the early days, not that
pounding pulse, not that fear that was a weapon; it
came later, tunneling through my bones.

I wouldn't have noticed, except he turned and saw me
watching.
"Mother," he said, his eyes filled up with
unspilled tears, "The bird was broken."

I wouldn't have noticed my fear, except then I knew,
the mother bird, for all her desperate beating of the
air, was powerless to save her child.

THIS I HID FROM JOSEPH

"I will never work with wood," he said.
A boy then, twig thin, brown, with eyes like night.
Joseph was away building. He had hopes for the
family business. There was much he didn't know.
I held my tongue as women were made to do.

In the streets boys roamed freely, snatching what
they could.
"My friends," he said returning hours later.
Finding the bread gone, I knew.
His friends, ragged and shoeless, thin as starving
dogs. This I hid from Joseph.

I found him standing at the running stream where
women washed clothes, the lowering sun stinging
my eyes but not inflaming his.
"Come." I said, "Time to come in. Your father…"
"My Father is not here," he said, "I heard a voice."
This I hid from Joseph.

Found him also at the temple steps where men
argued in whispers. Was it "Rome" (Did I hear that
word?) Was it "Jewish?" (Did I hear that word?)
They growled, "Woman go your way and take
that pup!"
Pulled him away before they could strike.
This I hid from Joseph.

There was much he didn't realize. A kind man who
kept us fed and clothed.
After all, do men perceive the rush of ken that moves
from infant's heart to nursing breast?

A woman knows her child.
Wanted for him ordinary peace and love. Wanted
for him good work and friendship and a cup of wine.
Tried to believe it would be so. Tried to wish him
into our lives.
Until the day I glimpsed him in a pushing, shoving,
crowd of boys, urging him onward.
And then I saw as bright as high day, his garment
trailing light, threads unraveling with much use, but
trailing tiny flecks of brilliance in the road.

I went home then. Shut my door and wept.
Let him have it for a small season, I prayed. Let him
have raucous friends, and boy sweat, and laughter
and tussling in the dusty sun.

I must have always known.
A mother knows her child.

WALKING TOWARD DISASTER

I leave Bethany with them,
Walking toward disaster, into the den of the beast that
is Rome and her minions.
Fear walks with me rattling its bag of bones.

~~~

Below the room, we cook. The women always cook.
Our voices muted; scent of lamb is in the air. We bake
the bread. It moves toward darkness and our fires
smoke.

The city is in motion. We can hear the crowds; we
can hear the clank of steel on steel, metal on metal,
marching feet. Who will live? Who will be passed
over? Who will be chosen to die? They come close.
Not yet, I pray, oh God, not yet.

My hands shake. The kitchen space is crowded.
I pour the wine and somehow waste it on my clothes.
It is as red as blood and washes down my skirt. My
face is wet with tears. I wipe the spill as best I can.
The woman with the alabaster box works with us, and
others. Some I know, some unknown to me.

They call for us. The stairs are dark. Sun barely
reaching us, and almost gone. I stumble once and

nearly drop the meat, Magdalene behind me with her
tray of bread.
She knows. I know. The woman with the box knows.

I heard him say it was his burial anointing. I heard him
say that.

~~~

My hands tremble. I serve the meal, pour the wine.
He motions we should sit.
The others look their disapproval, but we sit on stools,
watching, my stained skirt showing. I watch my son.
The two who yearn for glory argue. His eyes are full
and then he shakes his head. His shoulders droop.

Why? I ask myself. His life drains out like water
through a sieve. Why pour it out upon your
simpleminded squabbles? Do you not know we have
run out of time? The minutes slip away with every
word you speak.

He passes them the bread and wine and beckons us to
join, and then he speaks. Remember me, he pleads, his
body broken and his blood spewed out. Remember this.

He tears a scrap of bread. I hold my breath.
He dips his bread and gives it to the one who never

really understood. I want to shout, "don't trust him!" but the gloomy one departs, and the nightmare has begun.

They sing a song of sorrow. Too late for mother's touch, I do not try. I watch them go, his back resigned, walking toward disaster.

The women murmur hope. They are bones knocking. And I am not consoled.
I am not consoled.

ONLY ONE VOICE

Hell is everlasting noise. I know that now.

I keep my silence, even with Magdalene, but still it talks to me, this demon vision. It never leaves my head. It visits me unbidden. I see it pulsate, breathing as if today, every crevice of his body, every rivulet of blood, every piece of ruined skin, every sound.

~~~

I stood at the edge of the crowd drowning in noise.
Yes I knew they would see me, those who decide who will live and who will die.
I knew they could take me. It would be so easy. I am small and female and somehow a threat to Rome.
They could take me to that death, but I had stepped into sheol. What they could do to me was none of my concern.

Over the voices of men turned beasts there was only one voice I heard that day.
Did I not know my own child's cry? Over and through the animal howls for blood,
I heard him.

Had I not carried him on my breast? Had I not given milk in answer to that cry?
I who heard his wailing at the death of friends, I who had seen him shake with grief at the passing of Lazurus, I too had wept at his weeping.

Did I not know my child's strangled, wretched effort
to speak? His sweet voice ragged and torn?

He called for drink. My body ached to answer. He
called for the God he had taught me to love, the God
at this moment I hated.

Through all the frenzy of a world gone wild, I heard
his voice. I heard him.

> I heard him
> cry
> out
> and I heard
> and I heard
> and I heard.

———

THE CENTURION'S SLAVE
WATCHES MARY

She does not know I look at her. I cannot stop
watching her. Only the gods know why.

She is alive with pain. That I know.
That I can feel.
She is one of many women who moan but she is silent.
Standing there she shrouds her face and
then exposes it again. The women keen and wail.

She is unprotected, her soul undressed as a tree
stripped by hailstorm, wind-blasted with pain;
her soul is a naked child in a sandstorm,
every grain a knife.

I cannot stop watching her. Only the gods know why.
She is only one of many women. She is different.
I hear her roaring silence.

They begin the hammering. The women wail.
She rocks forward, but rights herself.

The crowd takes pleasure in it.
Their roar is deafening.
The stink of their hatred is everywhere.

The hammering continues.
She stumbles, straightens herself.
A woman strokes her back.

She shields her face once more. I grieve.
I think to never see her eyes again.

The man they hate is dying. And then again she pulls
away the mantle from her face.
Am I the only one who hears the noiseless fury
of her scream?

She cannot bear not to see. She stares at him
and he looks back in naked sorrow.
And then I know. Their faces are the same.
I see them. They are one.
I cannot stop watching.
My master summons. I must go.

Something I saw that will forever linger.
Her midnight black eyes meeting his,
and then he called for God and then he died.

I had to come away; my master called.
I could not stop watching her.
Only the gods know why.

THE LAST GIFT

I

In the beginning the sun burned fire through
my thin headdress, a ruthless heat.
I ate tears and sweat together.
Dogs followed the crowd. I knew what I would have
to do. They would not have his body.
Not one piece of him. Not one.

We climbed and climbed and every time he fell I
prayed that he would die. "Die now," I thought.
"Die now, my love, Oh please, my son, die now!"

I needed him to see me there. All I could give him
was my standing. That I would resist. That they would
not silence me, frighten me away. That what he could
endure, I could endure. That I would
keep the dogs from him. My last gift being there.

And so I stood. I would not move.
Dogs prowled the crowd.

When they nailed him, I stood.
When he saw me, I stood.
When he cried out, I stood.

Heaven's blue turns to slate.
A great knife rips the sky in two.

And black rain whips us all.
He breathes his last.
My bones are hollowed out, and finally,
I fall.

II

They tried to move me. Someone whispered in my ear,
"Come away," they said, "Come away; they will
see you."
I ran then, straight to him.
"I must keep the dogs away," I shrieked.
"I must keep the dogs from him!"
They tried to drag me off. "I am his mother!"
I raged.
"It is my right to wash and ready him!"

Women hold me. We are in the rain for hours.
His wounds are God-washed by the One he loved.
Gentle Joseph helps to take him down, my only one,
myself.
It rains. Who knows if it is Shabbot still? It rains.
The sky is black. I follow to the tomb.

~~~

They say He came to them. They say He left His
shroud and spoke to them. I let them carry on. I am
told something I know.
That He is here with me.
That He is always here.
That He is everywhere and everything.

Easter Day, April 20, 2014

*"But Mary Kept All These Things and
Pondered Them in Her Heart"*

~~~~~~

NO ONE HAS WRITTEN WHAT LURKS IN MY BONES

No one has written what lurks in my bones.
No one has told the story that lives inside me.
Does that mean it didn't happen?

No one has written that the day he died
the moon turned her face away for three days.
Does that mean it didn't happen?

No one has told of the black shadow that leans over
my narrow bed
and swallows my comfort
again and again, night after night.

And yet they sit in my house and argue
and wrangle, and dispute over the story they say
must be told.
No one has written that I have lost my love of trees
and that the wood grain bleeds when I look too hard.
I cannot tell that. No one would listen, and more,
they would cry madness.

The one he loved, she tells me to speak it.
I cannot make marks on the parchment as she can.
She tells me she will speak it if I don't.

She is fearless and white hot with willfulness.

When she speaks to them I see stars flashing fire,
and I know why he loved her.
She will not live long. This I know.

No one has written what I see.
They will write the story they do not know
For they have not asked me what I knew,
That the God he loved was not going to reach down
and keep the dogs asleep.
No, I said, I cannot tell it, all that was in my head,
all that I knew,
Only a woman, only a mother.

They have never asked me.
It is not my story they want.
It is theirs.
So I wait, my heart a stone that aches,
each breath a knife of remembrance.

So I wait, like waiting for his birth,
it feels never-ending, the promise of his kingdom
in my dreams.

THE LIGHT I SAW

A muted lamp casts shadows in my space, the oil almost gone,
and memories sit with me, alive.
I pray they leave me not, for they are all I have.

No one saw the light I saw, his eyes lit up with flame.
No one heard the thunder that was in my ears when he reached toward the sick.
No one saw the light I saw. It came to him at birth.
It is the same.
This was my son that I adored. This was my Lord.

~~~

I knew the look that came on him, I always knew.
A cloak of light that covered him, brilliant with love.
This blaze of sun that went into the sick and made them whole.
My heart shook and I trembled.

The old man at the pool praised God for his straight legs,
The blind man, how he sang that he could see.
The woman stopped her bleeding
and the man whose hand was healed.

I looked for those with hidden stones for they were always there, at the edges of the crowd, they hid stones in their sleeves. They waited.

It always stunned me when it came, his brightness. My ears were stopped. I watched the living fire; lame people walked again.
Then voices broke the silence. "Kill him! Kill him now! No such healing on the Shabbot! Not the law, not the law!"

~~~

I tell myself this sound is in my head now. I pull my shawl around my shoulders, tight.

~~~

I saw the star that came to us in childbirth go out from him to Lazarus. "Come out!" He called, in radiance like flame. My cousin stumbled, wrappings trailing in the dust. He was my son that I adored. He was my Lord.

~~~

I sit before my small flame by myself.
My heart in irons.
I sit before my oil lamp in the dark and wrap my shawl against the chill.
A gust of air puts out my light. I rest my head upon my hands.

It's over now, the press of bodies clamoring for help,
the glint eyed murderers who gather stones
and call for death,
their noise demanding that he love them.

He loved them and they hated that he loved them.
They are all gone and he is gone.
He was my son that I adored.

I sit in darkness. Moonlight on my table.

They have stolen my light.
God has stolen my Light.
I breathe and rest my head against my folded arms,
holding my heart together by my will alone.

It's over now, the raising of the dead, the panic of the
men, the soldiers and the blood.
It is gone and he is gone from me.
His brothers called him mad; they slandered him.
It was only that they did not see the Light I saw.
He was my son that I adored. He was my Lord.

I try to pray. Again I try to pray. Not comforted, I seal
my heart against my pain. I close my eyes. I sleep.

~~~

*I am a little child again. I see the temple steps all white
and glistening. I dance as they have taught me, the sky
above me nearly lapis blue. And then I see his sandals,
and look up. A man in royal robes is standing there. I
know him not. He calls me, Mother. "All is well," he
says. "Be at peace, Mother. All is well." I am adorned by
brilliance. I am washed in sun.*

~~~

Dawn comes. I go into my yard. I breathe the sun.
The sky is lapis blue. The sweetest flowers are in bloom.
I breathe his Love as if the dream is here.

The iron on my heart has gone away. I am at peace as
if the dream is here.
And then I know his Light has never left me.
He is my son that I adored. He is my Lord.

MARY IN WINTER

She walked the goat path, her stick tapping the dirt, the sorrow of centuries carried in her bent legs, pain that traveled the skeleton and entered the earth, reminding her how many years had gone since the blood time. Outside she talked only to herself and to her animals. There was no one else. The others were gone or dead. Inside her head she talked only to him to calm herself.

"The man you called my husband passed away," she said one day.

"He was not my Father," he would protest, *"My Father is in Heaven."*

It was never easy. Not in the early days, not later. Especially the remembering.

"Where is this Heaven you spoke of always?"

Silence

"So you left me for that?" She asked.

Stray dogs barked. She shook her stick at them.
"It would be easier if I didn't remember it all," she said.

"It will be better when you come home,"
He answered.

She knew he would say that. He always said that.

She knew this road, but the way seemed to be longer than ever. The caravan had left her alone. She stopped to get her breath. These days even breathing came hard. Her feet hurt. The worn out sandals were almost useless. The road was empty and that was good. Old women were always in danger.

Almost before the disappearing it had started. They whispered, they pointed. She was the mother of THAT ONE. They threatened, suggested fornication, stoning. They accused Magdalene, her only friend, of prostitution. That she was old now didn't matter. The law was the law. He was a criminal and so was she. They didn't crucify for nothing.

It was market day. No one else was going to the garden of tombs. She had chosen this way carefully. No curious strangers, thirsty for gossip.

More than half way there on the hill, she thought, "Did they even care, those friends of yours, what would happen to me? I am human after all!" She had said this to him more than once. She only thought it now.

"They loved you," He answered her thought.
"They did what they could."

"Well yes, John took me in," she said, "because you asked him to."

She had come to the stream and she drank, slowly bending her knees to the water, and wiping the sweat off her face with her long skirt. She stood up breathing heavily.

"I told you over and over," she said. "Walk this way and they will kill you. I knew it, and you knew it and still you were stubborn to the last!"

"That is why you bore me, my Mother," he said.

"I could have built a temple with the stones of my anger," she said "so great was my rage with you. It went into my bones this madness. It bent me. It nearly took my soul. If only we had stayed in Egypt. I did God's bidding! I bore you, frightened, and young and penniless. I fed you and petted you. How much more can I give? I did what He asked and still He took you from me!"

"Ah, but you will be with me in Paradise. This I know."

She had reached the place of what she called "the disappearing". The winter sun was out. She wanted to put her hands on the tomb, on that cruel stone, she

couldn't tell why, on that place where his body had
been laid down. Magdalene had seen an apparition
and some of the men, but she never did. He never gave
her that, only dreams. The tomb was empty and cold.
She laid her forehead on the surface of the entrance
and rubbed her hand over the unfriendly rock. And
when she heard him say,

"Come home,"

She caught one breath,
And then the darkness fell.

BEWARE THE MAN OF FIRE

They say if you look at the sun full on you will go
blind.
They never looked into his eyes.
They never could have.
Alive with Love he was a living target.
Beware the man of Fire.
There is no safety there.

Blinded by Love
You will stumble down his path and fall, silently,
splendidly,
Into a swirl of perfect knowing.

ACKNOWLEDGEMENTS

Special thanks to my dear friend Gabrielle Beard for her support, generosity, encouragement, vision, and sisterhood in the birthing of this message from the Mother.

Also, special thanks to Gloria Karpinski, sister/ friend and spiritual companion for her very kind words and her long- time belief in my writing.

Thanks to all my sister/friends, without whom I might have given up this journey a long time ago, and to my sister Barbara who is always an inspiration. Thanks also to my mother and to my sister who are in Spirit, for giving the very best they had always.

And thank you to my beautiful children, Chris and Willa, grandchildren Karrah, Kendall, Christopher, and to Adrian, Michael, and Christopher Foster who have taught me so much about mothering and to my husband, Gerald who stands by me always.

And finally to the Divine Mother of us all without whom none of this would have been possible, *Deo Gratias.*

You can find more information at:

www.lindabeatricebrown.com

www.womenandwisdom.com

Facebook:

Women and Wisdom Press

Linda Brown

ABOUT THE AUTHOR

Linda Beatrice Brown has taught at Kent State University, UNC-Greensboro, Guilford College and Bennett College. A graduate of Bennett College, she is recently retired as the Willa B. Player Distinguished Professor of the Humanities at her alma mater. She is the author of three novels, *Rainbow 'Roun Mah Shoulder*, *Crossing Over Jordan* and *Black Angels.*

Linda has been a guest lecturer at many schools, colleges and in cities throughout the country. She has poetry in several anthologies and magazines. Her last book, *Belles of Liberty*, was the story of Bennett College women's participation in the Civil Rights movement, published in 2013.

Linda has had three of her plays performed in North Carolina. Her novel *Black Angels* was the 2009 "Okra Pick" for the South Carolina Independent Booksellers and was named one of the best books of 2009 by the Chicago Public Libraries. A sequel entitled, *Angel Tree*, will follow.

A long time spiritual seeker, Linda was a diversity trainer for the Episcopal Church for many years. She has two adult children, and six grandchildren. She lives with her husband, Gerald White, in Greensboro.

CPSIA information can be obtained at www.ICGtesting.com
Printed in the USA
BVOW05s0106240216

437836BV00005B/9/P